Clevedon Court

North Somerset

THE NATIONAL TRUST

So lies the Court House, grey and still.
Surrounded by its lawns and flowers,
Beneath the sheltering woodland hill,
And basking in the summer hours....
A home of beauty and of grace,
In whose device of beam and stone
The perfect outline you may trace
Of social life in ages gone.

REV. J.E. COULSON, 1866

A HOME OF BEAUTY AND OF GRACE

'SITUATED on dry ground at the foot of a south-facing hill, with extensive views, just a couple of miles from the sea and with easy access to Bristol….' An imaginary estate agent's description of Clevedon Court's location suggests why the Norman family of de Clevedon in the 13th century chose this place to build a handsome manor house.

Three families have dominated the 700-year history of Clevedon Court, and its history reflects their fortunes. The house is still in essence the de Clevedons' medieval manor with its fine Great Hall and remarkable small chapel, remodelled in Tudor times by the Wake family, and further modernised in the 18th and 19th centuries by the Elton family.

The Eltons rose to riches and influence with the flourishing of 17th-century Bristol, and the stories of Clevedon Court and Clevedon town are interwoven with ten generations of this formidable family of entrepreneurs, merchants, country squires, intellectuals and artists. These are the very rooms that poets knew, the very chairs where the Merchant Venturers of Bristol sat, the very terraces that witnessed the tears, laughter and dreams of the passing generations. There are few aspects of local life that have not felt the Eltons' improving touch. Clevedon owes its development as a seaside resort to the vision and energy of the family.

Although the National Trust took over the ownership of Clevedon Court in 1960, the Elton link remains unbroken. The family still live in and love the home of their ancestors; when the doors are closed to the public, they move back into the Great Hall, bedrooms and gardens. The house is still filled with Elton furniture and pictures, reflecting the tastes, enthusiasms and achievements of ten generations.

You are welcome to visit the most significant rooms of the house and all of the gardens. On the hillside above, you can explore the maze of paths leading up through woodlands to views from Court Hill. This guidebook can give only a taste of the fascinating story of Clevedon Court, but the room stewards are happy to answer your questions, and 'room sheets' offer more detail on particular aspects of each room.

The Elton family and the National Trust hope that you will enjoy exploring Clevedon Court and its surroundings, and finding out about the people who lived here.

Far left The Clayton & Bell stained glass was installed in the Chapel after the fire of 1882

Left Family portraits cover the lofty walls of the Great Hall

Below The south, or entrance, front

3

1066–1432 THE DE CLEVEDONS
Lords of the medieval manor of Clevedon

The Manor of Clevedon was acquired at the Conquest by a Norman family. By about 1150 the de Clevedon family owned the manor, building a small manor house in the 13th century (now the Old Great Hall). About 1320 Sir John de Clevedon incorporated the old house within his imposing new manor house, the core of Clevedon Court as we know it today. The de Clevedon line died out in 1376, and the manor passed through female marriages to the Wake family.

1432–1630 THE WAKES
Wealthy Northamptonshire landowners

Roger Wake and his son, John, remodelled and enlarged the medieval house, putting in larger windows, fireplaces, a new west wing (now demolished) and new rooms on the north side. The Wakes sold the house and estate to the 1st Earl of Bristol in 1630.

1630–1709 THE EARLS OF BRISTOL AND CAREW RALEGH

The house and estate were confiscated from the 1st Earl of Bristol by Parliament during the Civil War, when it was handed over to Carew Ralegh, son of the famous Sir Walter. It was recovered in 1660 by the 2nd Earl and sold by the 3rd Earl in 1698.

1709– THE ELTON FAMILY
Dynasty of Bristol merchants and Somerset gentry

Clevedon Court was bought in 1709 by Abraham Elton, a Bristol merchant who made a fortune from the Bristol brass industry and other enterprises. He was created baronet in 1717 by George I. His son, Abraham II, modernised the house and grounds. Ten generations of Elton baronets owned Clevedon Court and extensive estates in Clevedon (see p.24). The house and grounds underwent periodic alterations until end of the 19th century.

The family wealth declined in the 20th century. On the death of the 9th Baronet in 1951, the high cost of repairs and heavy death-duties put the future of the house in jeopardy. The 10th Baronet worked closely with the Society for the Protection of Ancient Buildings, and a substantial grant for repairs was made. In 1957–60 the house was renovated and the victorianised west wing and additions on the north side demolished. The Treasury agreed to accept the house in part-payment of death-duties, and in 1960 it was passed to the National Trust.

CLEVEDON COURT, ESTATE AND TOWN
The house and its locality

The owners of Clevedon Court have always been central to local life and institutions, a tradition maintained by the present generations of Eltons. With the decline of Bristol as a port, the Eltons turned their attention to their Clevedon lands. The 5th Baronet, the Rev. Sir Abraham, was the first member of the family to live permanently in Clevedon and it was he who began to develop the town in the 1830s. The family coffers received a welcome boost from the sale of development land, but the Eltons also gave back to the town they were creating. In particular, Sir Abraham's grandson, Sir Arthur, 7th Baronet, devoted his life to Clevedon, masterminding the provision of fresh water and gas lighting, new churches, schools, a cottage hospital and the famous pier.

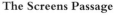

The Screens Passage
A taste of the Middle Ages

The Screens Passage was the spine of the medieval house and is the least changed part of Sir John de Clevedon's building. It separates the Great Hall, entered through double doors in the screen on the west side, from the service rooms entered through three arched openings on the east side. This layout is typical of a medieval manor house. However, the arrangement of the service rooms through these archways has changed over the centuries. The left-hand arch, which today opens into a corridor, originally led to the pantry, where the bread was kept. Through the middle arch, which now gives on to a 19th-century staircase leading to the nurseries, a passage would have led to the kitchen, while the right-hand arch would have led to the buttery, now the Justice Room (p.16).

THE ENTRANCE PORCH
You enter Clevedon Court by the south porch through the doorway built by Sir John de Clevedon, Lord of the Manor of Clevedon, in the most up-to-date style of the early 14th century. Beyond the south porch the stone-flagged Screens Passage leads to the north porch. Beside each door you can see portcullis grooves and the spiral, or newel, staircases that lead to the portcullis rooms above, where the windlasses to raise and lower them would have been. The heavily studded front door with its portcullis is mid-19th-century, but the north door at the other end of the Screens Passage is the elegant 18th-century one put there by the Eltons.

The Screens Passage is the least altered part of the house

7

The Great Hall
Heart of the house for seven centuries

Dining and living in a medieval household

When Sir John de Clevedon built his manor house in the 14th century, this room was much the same shape and size as now, but dark, draughty and smoky. It would have been open to the rafters and smoke from a central hearth found its way out by smoke-holes, which fed into the two castellated chimneys at the gable ends of the hall, visible from the garden. Small glassless windows at a lower level would have been protected by heavy wooden shutters, while a wooden screen separated the room from the Screens Passage to the east. The de Clevedons would probably have dined at the high table on a raised platform or dais at the west (far) end of the Hall, while their household ate less grandly at trestle tables. Beyond the magnificent pointed arch is an alcove and above it is the 'hanging' or first-floor Chapel. Over the arch you can see an internal window to the Chapel.

Tudor comforts

The medieval house would have been intolerably dark and cold by Tudor standards, and the Wakes set about rebuilding and extending it, adding a new west wing and several more rooms to the north of the building. The Great Hall is flooded with light from the windows they inserted, and in winter logs blaze in their Tudor fireplace. Note that the north window is directly over the fireplace. This unusual placing means that the chimney flue has to divide around it. The house owes much of its present-day appearance to the Wakes, whose contribution is commemorated by the Wake bears, their emblem, seen on the roof.

Eleven generations of Eltons

Today the Elton family still use the Great Hall for parties and musical evenings, and ten generations of baronets, their wives and families, look down from the walls. When the Eltons bought the house, they in their turn modernised it. We almost certainly owe the fine 18th-century plaster ceiling and screen to Sir Abraham II, while Sir Abraham IV added a pointed Gothic top with intersecting tracery to the great south window in the late 18th century. This was replaced about 1912 by Sir Edmund, 8th Baronet, who restored the window to something similar to its original Tudor form. The 19th-century Eltons put in central heating and gas lighting. Unusually, the house remained gas-lit until the Petroleum Board installed electric light in some of the main rooms, when they leased the house during the Second World War. However, Sir Ambrose, 9th Baronet, insisted on retaining gas light in his own apartments, which remained unmodernised until his death in 1951.

Each generation had its own tastes in furnishings and decorations; brown paint, flock wallpaper, panelling and elaborate draperies have come and gone (see above left).

Above The Great Hall in the late 19th century, when much of the stonework was covered in thick brown paint to imitate oak panelling

Right The 6th Baronet interrogates a suspected poacher in this picture by his son Edmund. It imagines the Great Hall as it might have looked before the Eltons put in the plaster ceiling in the 18th century

At the centre of life in the house since the Middle Ages, the Great Hall is still used as a family room. In spite of many changes through the centuries, it remains a fine example of a medieval manor hall.

As elsewhere in the house, the furniture in the Great Hall has been accumulated, used and treasured by a succession of Eltons. Some of it may have been left in the house by previous owners, such as the massive (and much altered) Tudor dining-table and the elaborately carved chairs, some ornamented with crowns, dating from the Restoration of Charles II.

Left The Great Hall today

Top Queen Victoria and her family depart for Scotland in the 1850s

Above Gurney's New Steam Carriage, 1827. Goldsworthy Gurney pioneered this early form of motorised transport, before the railway killed off the whole concept

Right The fine pointed archway with its carved heads to the left of the Thackeray Room stairs was revealed after the fire of 1882. It is part of the 14th-century house and would have formed the entrance to the de Clevedons' Solar or Great Chamber

The Queen Anne Staircase and Thackeray Room Landing

This elegant staircase was one of the improvements made by the 18th-century Eltons, and its fine window is the only survival of the fashionable architectural Gothick features they added to the house.

Today, the staircase is hung with 18th- and 19th-century prints of bridges, railways and canals. These formed part of a unique collection of books, illustrations and commemorative artefacts describing the rise of the Industrial Revolution and the social changes it brought about. The collection was made by Sir Arthur Elton, 10th Baronet, a distinguished pioneer documentary film-maker and writer with a lifelong passion for the history of technology. He described his collection as 'the history of how people looked at and thought about the railways and canals and bridges and factories that transformed the face of our country'. The main bulk of it was passed to the nation in lieu of death-duties in 1976 and is now at the Ironbridge Gorge Museum in Shropshire. This small portion was retained at the request of the National Trust as part of the history of the house and the Elton family.

Above Sir Arthur, 10th Baronet, filming during the 1930s

Left The Clifton Suspension Bridge. Sir Abraham, 5th Baronet, had shares in the Clifton Suspension Bridge Company. His second wife laid the foundation stone on the Clifton side in 1831

Top Jane Octavia Brookfield; by Albert Ludovici. She was the model for several of Thackeray's heroines

Above Tennyson as a young man

Right Arthur Hallam

The Thackeray Room
Literary connections and family tragedies
This little room, with its portraits of the Hallams, Tennyson and the Brookfields, commemorates the Eltons' 19th-century literary connections. The most famous of these is the friendship between Arthur Henry Hallam and Alfred Tennyson.

Hallam and Tennyson
Arthur Hallam was the son of the historian Henry Hallam and his wife Julia, the favourite daughter of the Rev. Sir Abraham Elton, 5th Baronet, and the Hallams frequently stayed at Clevedon Court. Years later, Arthur Hallam's cousin, Lucy Caroline Elton, remembered sliding down the side of the Queen Anne staircase with him. Arthur Hallam and Tennyson met at Cambridge in 1829, when they competed for the Chancellor's Gold Medal for English Verse, and Arthur later became engaged to Tennyson's sister, Emily. In 1833 Arthur Hallam died of a brain haemorrhage while in Vienna with his father. His death shattered his family and friends, particularly Tennyson, who almost immediately began to write what became 'In Memoriam. A.H.H.'. Recognised as the greatest elegy in the English language, it was Queen Victoria's favourite poem. There are many allusions to Clevedon in it, for Arthur's body was brought back to Clevedon Court and then carried through the streets of the town by the Eltons' tenants to St Andrew's church, where it was interred in the family vault. Tennyson himself stayed at Clevedon Court when he visited Arthur Hallam's resting place in 1850 on the publication of 'In Memoriam'. Although Arthur was only 22 when he died, he was considered by his friends, including William Gladstone, to be the most brilliant man they had ever known. In every generation of the Elton and Tennyson families, there have been children named Hallam in honour of their friendship.

Jane Brookfield and Thackeray
The other great literary friendship remembered here is that between William Makepeace Thackeray and Jane Octavia Brookfield, eighth daughter (hence her second name) of Sir Charles Abraham Elton, 6th Baronet. Jane (or Jenny, as she was known in the family) was married to the Rev. William Henry Brookfield, a close friend of Thackeray and Tennyson at Cambridge. Thackeray's wife suffered from mental illness and was confined in care, and he spent much time with Jane and her husband during the 1840s. In 1848, when Thackeray was visiting Jane at Clevedon Court, she is believed to have confessed to him her unhappiness with her marriage and Thackeray to have declared his love for her – tradition says on the Pretty Terrace, which you can see from the window. Their association came to an end in 1852 (it has always been said in the Elton family that Jane's uncle-in-law, Henry Hallam, who was devoted to her, offered her an annuity to break off her friendship with Thackeray). But both she and Brookfield live on in the pages of Thackeray's novels. Amelia Sedley in *Vanity Fair* and Lady Castlewood in *Henry Esmond* were both in part modelled on Jane, while Brookfield appears as the Rev. Charles Honeyman in *The Newcomes*.

THE STATE ROOM LANDING

This landing once opened into the corridor to the west wing, which the Wakes added in Tudor times. The paved terrace below the window indicates where the west wing used to stand. It included drawing room, dining room, great bedroom and several other bedrooms. The west front of this wing was constantly rebuilt, reflecting changing architectural tastes, from Tudor (*c.*1570), through Strawberry Hill Gothick (1760s), to Victorian Tudor (1860s), and was finally remodelled after a fire in 1882. It was demolished in the late 1950s, thus restoring the house to its medieval ground plan.

Left A charcoal study of Thackeray by J.E. Boehm for his fine statuette of the writer

The impressive State Room, still used occasionally as a guest bedroom, was one of the most important parts of Sir John de Clevedon's manor house. As the Great Chamber, or Solar, it was the Lord of the Manor's retiring room, where he slept, relaxed and received visitors. It now has an eclectic mixture of furniture, ranging from 17th-century oak chests to elegant 18th- and 19th-century pieces.

Far right top The 6th Baronet fathered two sets of twins, portrayed together here by Thomas Barker of Bath. The elder pair were christened Caroline Lucy and Lucy Caroline, and the younger Catherine Maria and Maria Catherine

Far right centre The three youngest children of the 6th Baronet, including Jane Octavia Brookfield, holding her doll, and their adored dog, Rob Roy

Far right below The Travellers' Breakfast; by Edward Villiers Rippingille, 1824. It includes portraits of the Eltons and many of their literary friends

The State Room
Medieval Solar and grand Victorian bedroom

In 1882 a beam in the chimney caught fire, and the ensuing blaze virtually destroyed the west wing. Furniture and pictures were burned, together with many irreplaceable books in the Library beneath, despite the efforts of the family, servants and villagers, who flung what they could out of the windows. The oak panelling around the fireplace came from the Eltons' former Bristol house in Queen Square and was acquired when it was demolished in the late 19th or early 20th century. The windows on either side were inserted after the removal of the west wing.

Sir Charles Abraham Elton, 6th Baronet, and his children

Many of the pictures in this room portray the family of Sir Charles Abraham, 6th Baronet (1778–1853), and his family, including a fine set of portraits of his wife, Sara, and eleven of their children. Sir Charles had been forbidden by his clergyman father from marrying the beautiful Sara Smith, daughter of a Nonconformist Bristol merchant, and was disowned by the family when he disobeyed. He consequently lived in comparative penury, earning his living as a journalist and classical scholar, publishing successful translations of Greek and Latin authors. A friend of many well-known literary figures of the day, he was also a poet. His best-known poem, 'The Brothers', was written after his two eldest sons were drowned at Weston-super-Mare in 1819.

When Sir Charles finally inherited in 1842, he had little interest in running a large estate and his son, later Sir Arthur Hallam Elton, 7th Baronet, almost immediately began to administer it for him. However, the sociable and witty Sir Charles brought the house alive with exuberant family parties and memorable Christmas celebrations.

Sir Charles's family and many of his literary friends appear in *The Travellers' Breakfast* (behind the door to the landing), which was painted in 1824 by another friend, the well-known Bristol artist Edward Villiers Rippingille. It shows a party shortly to depart on the stagecoach waiting outside. Sir Charles's eldest daughter, Julia, ogled by the poet Robert Southey, pours the tea, while her father looks on grinning from the fireplace. On the extreme left, Julia's mother, Sara, dressed as a poor widow, clasps the young Elton boys, Arthur Hallam and Edmund William, and family tradition says that the other girls are also Elton children. Charles Lamb hands a bill to Rippingille seated beside Wordsworth, who is smelling an egg held out by Coleridge, while Dorothy Wordsworth sits in stony silence with folded hands. Other well-known contemporaries who are also thought to appear in the picture include the writers Leigh Hunt and John Clare.

The Chapel

The Chapel next to the State Room is part of John de Clevedon's manor house. It would have been used only by the Lord of the Manor and his immediate family, while the rest of the household had prayers in the Great Hall below.

The finest architectural feature of Clevedon Court is the remarkable south window of the Chapel with its reticulated tracery. Of unusual rectangular shape, it dominates the front elevation of the house. The Chapel was originally dedicated to St Peter and was probably used for worship until the Wakes' alterations of the 16th century, the period when the east window may have been concealed and the room panelled. Its use as a chapel was forgotten for the next 300 years, when it served as a study, dressing room and boudoir. It has always been said in the family that Thackeray wrote part of *Henry Esmond* in it.

The Chapel was badly damaged in 1882 by the fire which started in the State Room chimney. During the subsequent restoration, the builders uncovered much unsuspected medieval stone-work, including the blocked east window and the remains of a medieval altar and piscina (basin). The room was restored as a chapel, and rededicated to All Souls. The clear glass had been destroyed in the fire, and the present stained glass was made by the well-known Bristol firm of Clayton & Bell.

The Justice Room
now the Glass Room

700 years ago, this room was the buttery of Sir John de Clevedon's manor house, where the beer butts would have been stored. Later, wrong-doers would have waited here to come before a manorial court in the Great Hall, hence the name 'Justice Room'. In the 19th century, during the time of the 7th and 8th baronets, it served as a gun-room and during the Second World War was used as a dining room by the 9th Baronet and his wife, no doubt because it was smaller, and therefore warmer, than other rooms in the house.

Nowadays the room houses the fine collection of 19th-century glassware amassed by Dame Dorothy Elton, wife of the 9th Baronet, and her younger son, Ralph. Some of the pieces were made just four miles away at the Nailsea Glass Works, which produced large quantities of window and bottle glass, as well as utilitarian items such as rolling-pins and cucumber straighteners, which you will see in the collection, while the hats were probably apprentice pieces. Although true Nailsea glass is plain green, the term 'Nailsea Glass' has come to be used for much coloured and decorative glass of the 19th century, such as the flasks, pipes and fancy lampwork groups of bird fountains and ships, which were more likely to have been made in Sunderland or Stourbridge in the Midlands.

Top The fine groups of birds with their spun-glass tails are spectacular demonstrations of the glass-workers' technical mastery

Above Nailsea glass stirrup flasks

Right Nailsea glass rolling-pins in the Justice Room

Far right The Chapel was used as a boudoir until the fire of 1882 revealed the hidden east window, when it was restored to its original use

The Old Great Hall

Studio pottery in an ancient building

The left-hand archway in the Screens Passage, which gave on to the pantry of the medieval house, now leads into a passageway to a small courtyard – the 'Pump Court'. The pump is above a well, once the house's water supply. The medieval walls of the courtyard are a confusing jigsaw of stone and brick, with many puzzles of chronology and function.

The first manor house

Beyond the courtyard is the oldest part of Clevedon Court – a much smaller manor house, which predates Sir John de Clevedon's grand building of 1320 by perhaps 50–80 years. For six and a half centuries, the Old Great Hall was used as a kitchen (and is sometimes still known as the Old Kitchen), but in the 13th century it was the home of the Lord of the Manor of Clevedon and his family and household. The Hall was open to the rafters, with a central hearth, and buttery and pantry at the northern end.

During its history the Old Great Hall has seen many changes. In Tudor times the Wakes added the fireplace and chimney, and you can see bread ovens and a salt cupboard. By 1957, on the death of Dame Dorothy, when the room ceased to be used as a kitchen, the old range had long since been replaced by an Aga.

Eltonware

Today, the Old Great Hall is used as a museum to display the splendid studio or 'art' pottery made from the 1880s by Sir Edmund Elton, 8th Baronet, who inherited Clevedon Court in 1883. He was a gifted inventor, but pottery became his passion. In the late 1870s, he set up workshops and a kiln in outbuildings beyond the stables and taught

himself to throw pots, assisted by the hunch-backed George Masters, whom he had taken on straight from school. 'Eltonware', as it came to be known, vividly reflects Sir Edmund's creative and original approach to glazing, colour and form, though as he himself modestly put it, 'If an ignorant country baronet set out to make mud pies and didn't know anything about it, and used plenty of glazing, he was bound to turn out something queer.' He used the famous New York firm of Tiffany as one of his agents, and Eltonware became internationally recognised.

Sir Edmund was greatly loved in Clevedon, lavishly entertaining the townspeople. However, changes in farming and taxation began to diminish the family's wealth, a fate that befell many other landed families at the time, and it was he who sold many of the farms, cottages and other land that had supported the family and house.

The Tower

The Tower stands at the extreme east end of the house. Tall and four-storeyed, with thick walls, arrow-slit windows and a severe façade, it has always been thought to be the oldest part of the building, predating the main house. However, after careful re-examination of the building, this is now being reconsidered, and it is perhaps part of the planned reconstruction of the 14th century.

THE GARDENS AND GROUNDS
Beautiful setting for an imposing house

'One of the noblest ranges of terrace walls in England' GERTRUDE JEKYLL, WALL AND WATER GARDENS, 1901

Above In the late 19th century the lawn below the terraces was formally planted with gaudy island beds

Right The Lower Garden about 1906, showing the elaborate and labour-intensive planting favoured by Sir Edmund and Dame Agnes

Far right The Pretty Terrace in 1899. Note the Eltonware roundel set into the Summer House

The dramatic architectural character of the garden, which rises steeply back in a series of terraces carved out of the hillside, is not immediately apparent from the front of the house but it offers a memorable experience that should not be missed.

The development of the garden

The garden is first described in 1629, as 'two gardens, an orchard, a fayre court, a strong and large barne, and other out houses, besides 60 acres of wood and coppice'. The *c.*1720 bird's-eye view (front cover) shows the fine pilastered wall of the Pretty (middle) Terrace as it exists today. This wall was probably built by the Eltons after they bought the estate in 1709, though it may have replaced an earlier boundary wall.

In the mid-18th century, Sir Abraham IV made substantial changes to the garden when he was gothicising the house, and it is still essentially in the form laid out by him. He demolished the boundary wall to the west and put in the double flight of brick steps which gives such grace to this side of the garden. He extended the Pretty Terrace to the west, terminating it with the fine Octagon at one end and a simple summer-house at the other (Sir Edmund added Eltonware panels to both buildings, only removed in the 1960s). The bird's-eye view shows a doorway at the east end of the Pretty Terrace, which once gave access to the bare hillside behind, and you can see its arched top in the wall today. However, Sir Abraham IV filled in this doorway and back-filled behind the wall to form the Top, or Wild, Terrace.

The best description of the early 19th-century garden appears in Sir Charles Abraham I's 1819 poem, 'The Brothers':

I stood upon a lawn whose greensward spread
Smooth-levell'd by the scythe; two mulberry trees
Beyond it stretch'd their old and foliaged arms;
　　　　　　　　　… the mansion's walls,
Grey in antiquity, were tapestried o'er
With the fig's downy leaves, and roses climb'd
Clust'ring around the casements' gothic panes
With terraces and verdant slopes, where pines
Arch'd their plumed boughs, and fruits espalier-train'd
Were mix'd with myrtles and with arbute-trees.

In the early years of the Trust's ownership, its chief garden expert, Graham Stuart Thomas, worked closely with Lady Elton, wife of the 10th Baronet, and Patricia Elton, wife of his younger brother, Ralph. It was decided to simplify the planting with emphasis on rare shrubs and trees, rather than elaborate herbaceous bedding, so that it could be maintained by one permanent gardener with intermittent assistance. This policy is continued by the present generation of the family.

Photographs of the Edwardian garden show its fussy, high-maintenance bedding schemes, deplored by Gertrude Jekyll, who criticised the small square beds along the Pretty Terrace and was horrified by 'the most commonplace' planting at the foot of the brick wall of the lowest terrace. What was left of this was swept away during the 1960s. Most of the kitchen gardens and Victorian greenhouses to the east of the car-park were sold in the late 1950s to pay death-duties.

21

Top The Pretty Terrace

Above The lawn to the west of the house

Right The terraces in early spring. The Round House appears on the *c.*1720 bird's-eye view

The garden today

From the back of the house you enter the garden up a flight of formal steps. These cut through the lowest retaining wall to curving paths, from which the lawn rises gently past the central fountain, a remnant of the Victorian garden. On the east (right-hand) side, the garden is bounded by an ancient, castellated wall punctuated by the Round House, but on the west side the boundary is more subtle, formed by a screen of trees, which separates this formal space from the open slope beyond. Above the fountain a steep bank rises to the lowest terrace with its much-restored 18th-century rose-pink brick wall. The Pretty and Wild Terraces are reached either by another flight of steps to the east or via a grove to the west with winding steps and paths, shaded by a great magnolia tree.

Stand and look down the length of the Pretty Terrace, enclosed by Sir Abraham IV's garden pavilions at either end, before strolling back and forth along its length. At one end of the terrace you see the formal walled garden and the back of the house with its jumble of gables, so different from the stately massiveness of the entrance front. At the other end, there is a completely different view, leading the eye down the long slope of the West Bank to the Lower Garden, which is informally planted with great trees, and out over the wide vista of the misty and mysterious moors to the Mendip Hills beyond.

From the height of the Wild Terrace you can catch a glimpse of the Bristol Channel glinting to the south-west. In the Edwardian garden a symmetrical line of evergreens was planted in an attempt to mark the transition from formal garden to informal woodland. Today, all thought of formality has been abandoned here, and the Wild Terrace now lives up to its name. It has been allowed to melt naturally back into the woods behind, though the self-seeded evergreen oaks at the east end are being cut back to reveal a romantic, craggy rock-face.

Court Hill

For centuries, Court Hill behind Clevedon Court was open common land grazed by sheep, but in 1801 an Enclosure Act allowed Sir Abraham V to plant it with trees as an investment, while his second wife laid out ornamental walks with stone steps, rustic seats and small bridges. Such was the pleasure that this must have given the Eltons and their guests that even in the austere 1920s, after Sir Ambrose, 9th Baronet, had dismissed most of the servants, there were still ten woodsmen to keep the hill paths open. Today, Sir Abraham V's 115,000 fir and larch have almost all gone, and the hillside is heavily wooded with holm, or evergreen, oak, but fragments of his wife's layout remain. Though the peace of garden and woods ended in 1973 with the opening of the motorway, you can still hear the buzzards mewing overhead.

Below The terraces

THE ELTONS OF CLEVEDON COURT

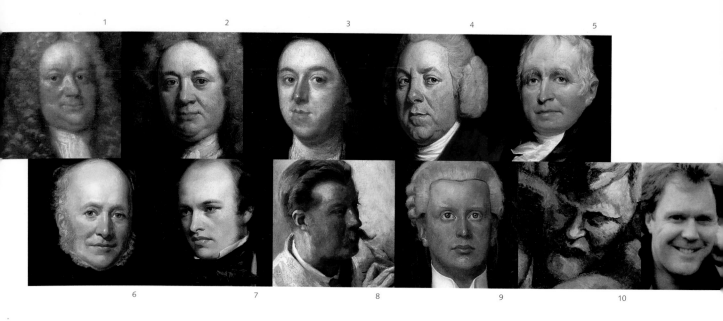

1   2   3   4   5

6   7   8   9   10

1 Sir Abraham I, 1st Baronet
(1654–1727) Immensely rich
and successful self-made Bristol
entrepreneur. Master of the
Merchant Venturers, Mayor of
Bristol, Member of Parliament;
made Baronet in 1717. Bought
Clevedon Court in 1709.

2 Sir Abraham II, 2nd Baronet
(1679–1742) Added to the family
fortunes. Member of Parliament.
Renovated and modernised
Clevedon Court.

3 Sir Abraham III, 3rd Baronet
(1703–61) Mayor of Bristol. Went
bankrupt in 1745, and the grand
Elton house in Queen Square
auctioned.

4 Sir Abraham IV, 4th Baronet
(1718–90) Younger brother of
3rd Baronet. Barrister, Master of
the Merchant Venturers, President
of the 'Gentlemen of Somerset'.
Town Clerk of Bristol, then a very
powerful civic position. Remade
family fortune. Remodelled west
wing, laid out gardens and built
the Octagon.

5 Rev. Sir Abraham, 5th Baronet
(1755–1842) The first Elton to live
permanently in Clevedon. His first
wife brought him substantial
Clevedon properties as a dowry,
and his second wife made many
changes to the house and gardens.
Began to develop the town of
Clevedon.

**6 Sir Charles Abraham I,
6th Baronet** (1778–1853) Writer,
classical scholar and poet. Thirteen
children. Brother-in-law of Henry
Hallam, friend of Charles Lamb,
Robert Southey, Walter Savage
Landor and other literary and
artistic figures.

7   **Sir Arthur Hallam I, 7th Baronet**
(1818–83) Victorian philanthropist.
JP. MP for Bath 1857–9. Planner,
developer and benefactor of the
town of Clevedon, putting in water
supply, sewers and public lighting
as well as building schools,
churches, the cottage hospital
and the pier. Altered the house
during the 1860s and twice rebuilt
the west wing.

8 Sir Edmund, 8th Baronet
(1846–1920) Self-taught innovative
studio potter. Entertained lavishly,
sold land to keep finances afloat.
JP and Chairman of Urban District
Council, founder and captain of
the Clevedon Fire Brigade.

9 Sir Ambrose, 9th Baronet
(1869–1951) Barrister, historian
and antiquarian. JP and Chairman
of Urban District Council. Inherited
heavily mortgaged estate and lived
in frugal style with his wife Dorothy,
a well-known and eccentric figure
in Clevedon.

**10 Sir Arthur Hallam II, 10th
Baronet** (1906–73) Pioneer
documentary film-maker, collector
and authority on the history of
technology. His efforts ensured the
survival of the house for the future
in the face of escalating costs of
repair and high death-duties.
Carried out extensive and urgent
repairs before passing Clevedon
Court to the National Trust in 1960.

**11 Sir Charles Abraham II, 11th
Baronet** (b.1953) Writer and TV
film producer. Together with his
young family, lives in London and
at Clevedon Court, as does his
sister, Julia.

24